EDWARDS COACHES
A HUNDRED YEARS

SIMON INGHAM

AMBERLEY

Acknowledgements

Edwards would like to thank the following people and organisations for contributing to this publication: former and current valued employees, suppliers, contractors and clients who have contributed to Edwards successes; individual contributors, in particular Mike Street, Peter Owen, Chris Morrish, Stuart Gerrish, Mike Taylor and the Cardiff Transport Preservation Group; extended thanks go to David Gray and Tudor Thomas for their input on A.B.S. and John Jones for content and proofreading; David Donati for fleet lists and buslistsontheweb.co.uk for support in the collation of vehicle details; author Simon Ingham, Richard Thomas and Nia Evans for pursuing this publication and other initiatives marking Edwards' centenary; resorts and locations used for photoshoots; and Amberley Publishing for releasing the title in Edwards' centenary year.

Whilst every attempt has been made to ensure accuracy, the author, Edwards and the publisher apologise for any errors. Whilst vehicle details are included within the captions, space limitations do not allow for a full history of each. For ease of reference and simplicity, 'Edwards' as an entity is used as the collective term for the Operator (not to be confused with the same or similar names). For presentation purposes, photos included within are organised in a loose date captured order and are duly attributed to the original photographer, where known.

First published 2025

Amberley Publishing
The Hill, Stroud
Gloucestershire, GL5 4EP

www.amberley-books.com

Copyright © Simon Ingham, 2025

The right of Simon Ingham to be identified as the Author of this work has been asserted in accordance with the Copyrights, Designs and Patents Act 1988.

ISBN 978 1 3981 2357 1 (print)
ISBN 978 1 3981 2358 8 (ebook)

British Library Cataloguing in Publication Data.
A catalogue record for this book is available from the British Library.

Typesetting by SJmagic DESIGN SERVICES, India.
Printed in Great Britain.

Foreword

It is a great honour to be writing this piece as Edwards Coaches marks 100 years since its entry into passenger transport in 1925. From humble beginnings, we have become the largest family-owned and independent public-transport operator in Wales and one of the largest in the UK. I am immensely proud of how far Edwards Coaches has developed – today we are synonymous with high-performing bus and coach travel. The fact that we are an award-winning and widely recognised company is down to the hard work and dedication of everyone that has been involved in Edwards Coaches over the past 100 years. I am eternally grateful for everyone's input in making Edwards Coaches the success that it is today. I would also like to thank every one of our customers for choosing Edwards Coaches and I look forward to continuing to serve our communities beyond 2025.

I sincerely hope that you enjoy the following pages, learning more about our rich history. The book features many great images of a wide variety of the vehicles that have operated with us over the years. Some vehicles, after their life with us, have gone on to serve with other operators or have entered the preservation scene. Some have become mobile shops, caravans and even support vehicles in war-afflicted countries.

It is unequivocal that a great deal has changed since 1925. Since then, we have seen twenty-one prime ministers, the opening of two bridges spanning the River Severn, a world war, the rise and fall of coal mining in Wales, joining the European Union and later leaving it, the invention of the internet, emails, personal computers and mobile phones, a health pandemic and many other significant world events. I wonder what founder George Edwards would think about today's world and the Edwards business? We've grown from being an operator of a handful of public-service vehicles to around eighteen vehicles in 1970, sixty vehicles by 2000 and over 250 vehicles today. Our front-line tour coaches have air conditioning, USB sockets, toilets and serveries onboard as well as advanced safety features and Euro 6 engines, a far cry from the very basic passenger-carrying vehicles of the 1920s.

Edwards Coaches has an extremely bright and positive outlook beyond 2025. We remain committed to delivering superior travel experiences, combining our heritage and vast industry experience with innovation to remain being recognised as a key player in the bus and coach industry in the UK.

Mike Edwards
Proprietor and Chairman

Introduction

Originally from Castle Martin in Pembrokeshire, the Edwards family moved to the Rhondda Valley during the late nineteenth century. Brothers George, William and James Edwards were heavily involved in the construction industry and built most of the houses in Clydach Vale, the Tonypandy Grammar School and the Judges Hall, amongst others. It is said that the family were tied to a contract to build houses for Powell Duffryn, who was developing a new coal mine in Tynant. The contract price was £80 for each house but this became unsustainable, particularly with the advent of the First World War and associated shortage of labour and materials. Contracts could not be fulfilled, and the building business became bankrupt during the depression that followed in the postwar years.

George and his family moved from Trealaw in the Rhondda to a small farm in Beddau, and this became the base for the new public-transport business. George and James ventured into transportation just after the First World War, operating goods vehicles to help sustain their building firm. They converted trucks (some ex-military) into passenger-carrying vehicles, an example being Daimler L5952, new in May 1915, being converted from a goods lorry to an eighteen-seat passenger vehicle and first registered as such in March 1921. In March 1925, George Edwards (or 'Father Edwards') applied to Pontypridd Urban District Council for a licence to operate between Beddau and Pontypridd. Though not the first passenger-transport company to operate this route, Edwards' licence was granted in May 1925, thus properly and formally marking their entry into their passenger-transport business.

Under the 1930 Road Traffic Act, licensing of bus routes and operators passed from local authorities to the Traffic Commissioners. From April 1931 licensing details appeared in 'Notices & Proceedings' (N&P), published weekly until September 1931 when publication became fortnightly. Existing operators were required to apply to continue to run their existing services. With very few exceptions, continuations were automatically granted. 'Edwards Bros' (named after George's three sons, James, Isaiah and Cyril), The Garage, Beddau, first appeared in N&P issue 3, dated 15 April 1931, no. TGR469.

Edwards Bros, together with the other companies such as Bebb of Llantwit Fardre, Palmer of Treforest, Gardner of Tonteg, Gray of Tonteg, Maisey of Church Village and Williams of Tynant, collaborated to form the 'Amalgamated Bus Service' (A.B.S.) to ward off competition from the Rhondda Tramways Company (Rhondda Transport Company from 1934) and South Wales Commercial Motors, later Western Welsh.

These operators were granted licences for the Pontypridd–Beddau route in N&P, dated May 1931, having formed the collective to improve the locality's public-transport offering. Private hires, charters, trips and tours were excluded from the agreements of A.B.S. and could operate at their own business discretion. A.B.S. had opened an office in Pontypridd and Gwyneth Edwards (wife of Isaiah) was one of the first secretaries. A.B.S. operated with coordinated times and fares. The first full year of pooled revenue (based on mileage operated) was 1926. To avoid accusations of irregular running, conductors had to clock in at various Bundy clocks along the route, for example, at The Three Horseshoes, Tonteg, and another opposite the Hollybush, Church Village. Penalties were enforced if operators ran late to poach passengers from the competing bus behind. 'Uncle Lyn' (the son of Gwyneth and Isaiah and much younger brother of Denzil and Alvis) recalled that if the bus was a minute early or late, the company would be fined 1s per minute.

N&P no. 85, dated December 1933, records the Edwards address as Ty Twarch, Beddau. N&P 179, dated May 1937, refers to the operator specifically as James, Isaiah and Cyril Edwards (George's descendants), trading as 'Edwards Bros'. The company entitled 'Edwards Bros (Beddau) Ltd' at Ty Twarch Farm was registered on 12 November 1942. However, as TGR3550, it only appeared in N&P no. 250, dated January 1947, as N&Ps were suspended for the duration of the Second World War when such matters were under the direct control of the Ministry of War Transport. During the war years, Edwards carried multiple workers to the munitions factory in Bridgend, a vital contribution to the war effort.

In the postwar period, Edwards carried workers to the booming Treforest Industrial Estate. The 1950s and 1960s saw an increase in the popularity of long-distance coach travel, with vehicles equipped with heaters and radios contributing to the appeal of this method of travel. Destinations such as Bath, Blackpool, Evesham, Stratford-upon-Avon and London were favourites. The first tours into Europe also took place in the 1960s with popular destinations including Ostend, Paris and Oberammergau, Germany, to see performances of Passion Plays. All these destinations continue to be served by Edwards.

Edwards' stage services passed to Bebb (Valaironny Ltd) in August 1969. The rest of the Edwards operation followed in June 1974 after Alvis Edwards' heart attack. Alvis had become the majority shareholder on the passing of Isaiah and subsequent acquisition of shares from Denzil and Lyn. The Edwards business continued to operate as a separate concern until the passing of licences to Bebb (TGR4057) in April 1975. Apart from the Edwards livery continuing under Bebb ownership, there was limited official Edwards presence until March 1976 when a new operation was recorded under the name of the recovered Alvis Edwards, Parish Road, Tynant. This operation became 'AG Edwards Travel Limited', based at Ty Twarch with four coaches.

Following a short hiatus in operations when AG Edwards Travel Limited was wound down and through encouragement from his father, Mike Edwards was granted operator licence PG5996 in June 1982, initially from a home address in Tonteg, but later recorded at Edwards' Garage, Ty Twarch, Beddau (August 1982). These were the same historical premises used prior to the takeover by Bebb in 1975 when the company Operated as 'Edwards Bros (Beddau) Ltd'.

Outgrowing the operational base at Ty Twarch, Edwards relocated to Atlantic Industrial Estate, Llantwit Fardre, between summer and November 1984. Atlantic Industrial Estate was renamed Newtown Industrial Estate in late 1991 and became the primary operational base for Edwards until its move to Parc Busnes Edwards. The Llantwit Fardre site was formerly occupied by Nova Oil and Solvent, a rag factory that processed old clothes to make wipers for the National Coal Board, local garages, Royal Ordnance factories and the Royal Navy, etc. Upon acquisition of the site, improvements to it began instantly. It grew from 4 to 8 acres through the purchase of the old Gilbern car factory in the late 1980s and the acquisition of the site occupied by Form and Surface Grinding Limited.

Edwards acquired the businesses of Alan Clough (Pontypridd), trading as Mayfayre Coaches, and John Galvin (Porth) in April 1984. A further acquisition came in 1993 in the form of Humphreys Coaches, Pontypridd, with three coaches (MUH 949P, C598 HTX and E321 TTX) and the goodwill of the business following the retirement of the owners. The business of Glyn Rees of Nelson trading as East Glam Motors Ltd (Nelson) with seven coaches was acquired in November 1989.

In July 1995, Grays Coaches of Pontypridd was acquired; the vehicles operated out of the Grays yard at Maesycoed, Pontypridd. By 1999, the owners of Atlantic Transport Services, the parent company of Edwards, went their separate ways and decided to sell the business. The accountants Grant Thornton were engaged to advertise the business for sale and to accept the highest secret bidder. Mike Edwards bid the highest and subsequently took full control, thus ending the 'Edwards & Ryan' period from 1992.

Edwards Coaches Ltd was incorporated in August 2000 with new licences being acquired initially under the name of Mike Edwards at Efail Isaf, PG0007476, then PG1044350 under the name of Edwards Coaches Ltd at Newtown Industrial Estate, Llantwit Fardre. The business thrived and numerous additional operating centres were established in the following decade.

On 12 April 2010, Edwards re-entered local bus-service work after a community plea for a better bus service in the area. It launched a half-hourly service, the 'Citylink' 400E, between Gwaunmiskin, Beddau and Cardiff. This was followed a week later by the high-frequency 'Ponty Dart' 100E, serving the Royal Glamorgan Hospital, Llantrisant, Beddau and Pontypridd. The letter 'E' accompanied the service number to distinguish it from the poor-performing incumbent operator, Veolia Transport Cymru, which had acquired Bebb. A period of intense competition followed. In retaliation, Veolia rebranded their 400 service as 'The Glider', the 100 receiving new vinyls denoting the service as 'one-hundred'. In June 2011, First Cymru registered a competing service on the 400 against both Edwards and Veolia, as well as extending their 44 service between Bridgend and Talbot Green to Pontypridd via Tonteg and Beddau. Anecdotal reports claim that passengers would let Veolia and First pull up at the bus stop and to then walk past their buses to board the favoured Edwards service. Veolia withdrew their services in June 2012 when the company restructured its Welsh operations. First subsequently withdrew its service, leaving the commercial routes 100 and 400 in the hands of Edwards.

Edwards initially acquired eight Wright Crusader-bodied Dennis Darts from Belfast and a trio of former Arriva North West Wright Endurance Volvo B10B-58s for the work. These were later supplemented by former Airparks MCV Evolution-bodied MAN 14.220s, an MCV Stirling-bodied MAN 14.220, Plaxton Primos, ex-Cardiff Bus Optare Excel (R209 DKG) and, surprisingly, an LDV Convoy (WA54 AFK). Edwards has since bought brand-new vehicles, including Alexander Dennis Enviro 200s, Enviro200 MMCs, MCV Evolution-bodied Volvo B7RLEs and MCV Evora-bodied Volvo B8RLEs, some pressed into service in base white livery prior to painting into Edwards colours. A rarity was to find Dennis Trident double-deckers (normally used on school-bus/Cardiff University contract duties) and occasionally coaches being used on its Cardiff runs for additional match-day capacity. Various interesting demonstrators have been used on local services over the years, too, including an Optare Solo, an Optare Tempo, an Optare Versa, a MAN 14.250 City Smart, a MCV-bodied Volvo B7LE, a Wright Streetlite WF and a few Mercedes-Benz Citaros, including BF68 ZHB, which later was acquired by Cardiff Bus.

Further and significant expansion followed in January 2011 through the acquisition of Diamond Holidays, Swansea, which had entered administration. Edwards purchased the firm's names (D. Coaches Ltd and Brian Isaac Coaches Ltd), goodwill and assets, including 2009-registered Bovas and Setras. This purchase greatly strengthened Edwards' position in Swansea. Edwards reported that it had sold nearly £1 million worth of holidays in the immediate aftermath and as a result drafted in additional staff to manage the volume of work. Edwards leased the former Diamond premises in Swansea Enterprise Park in the Llansamlet area of the city for a year before purchasing neighbouring land with a garage facility, which the company refurbished before transferring operations there.

In May 2011, Edwards took over National Express diagrams formerly operated by Veolia Transport Cymru. Eleven new Caetano Levante-bodied Volvo B9Rs were delivered for use on the scheduled network. The volume of National Express work expanded again in June 2012 as Edwards took over First Cymru's 202 Swansea to Heathrow journeys. This was supplemented in July 2012 with the remainder of First Cymru's diagrams, adding a total of sixteen additional Caetano Levante-bodied Volvo B9Rs to the fleet. The partnership with National Express continued to flourish with frequent investment in fleet replacement and the opening of a new depot in Bristol.

In 2013, Mike Edwards as the sole shareholder of Edwards Hotels Ltd, purchased the forty-four-bedroom Portbyhan Hotel in Looe, Cornwall, after the business had gone into administration. A full refurbishment of the exterior, bedrooms, restaurant, bar and public areas commenced on what is affectionately known as the 'Cornish Welsh Embassy'. The harbour-side location and the excellent services that the hotel offers post-renovation contributed to the Portbyhan Hotel winning accolades such as 'Best Individual Hotel' at the prestigious National Coach Tourism Awards.

Ten brand-new tri-axle Mercedes-Benz Tourismos arrived in March 2015. These introduced a new Tour livery that featured pink swirls on the metallic-blue base colour. All the vehicles were lined up outside Wales' Millennium Centre for a press launch, making an impressive sight during the company's commemorative ninetieth year. Costing £2.75 million, this investment contributed to Edwards winning 'Top Large Fleet Operator, 2015' at the UK Coach Awards, as well as 'Welsh Coach of the Year' at the UK Coach Rally for the third year running. Two of the batch were withdrawn early on due to unfortunate incidents. BJ15 AWM was hit in a multi-vehicle pile-up on the A2 near Lucerne, Switzerland, on 4 September 2015. This vehicle was subsequently purchased by ICoaches in February 2016 and returned to the road. BJ15 BCV caught fire on the M4 on 5 December 2015 whilst on a Christmas-market excursion.

From 2016 until 2020, Edwards operated school bus services and four local bus services after Silcox Motor Coach Company Limited ran into financial difficulties in Pembroke Dock. Edwards re-employed former Silcox staff, retained some Silcox vehicles and developed various operating centres. Waterloo Garage is still owned by Edwards, though currently leased to Taf Valley Coaches.

Also in 2016, Edwards bought the former 25-acre Fram Filter factory in Llantrisant under the name Dragonfruit Holdings Ltd. After considerable demolition and reconstruction work over a period of two years, Parc Busnes Edwards became the new home of Edwards Coaches from 2018. Located opposite the Royal Mint, it's an impressive 25-acre site boasting garage facilities, a customer park-and-ride facility and a spacious customer waiting room. Other units within the business park are leased by private tenants. The National Express operation moved there in 2017 as part of the strategic relocation from the former HQ in Llantwit Fardre.

In April 2017, Edwards opened a new depot at Moorend Farm Avenue in Avonmouth, Bristol, to fufil a new ten-year contract for National Express in the South West under associated licence PH2001471. A new fleet of National Express vehicles came with it, as well as National Express-owned Boa Vista double-deckers, supplementing the already long-standing National Express contract held by Edwards in South Wales. Edwards was the first of National Express' partner operators to run Caetano Levante 3s, BU18 OTF being amongst the first of the type.

In April 2019, ten charities won the opportunity to have free advertising space on the back of an Edwards' vehicle for a year via a social-media competition. The original intention was to have four winners on four vehicles for a duration of three months. However, eighty-four submissions were made and consequently Edwards extended the number of winning entries to ten.

Jean Edwards, Mike Edwards' mother, passed away on 27 May 2019, aged ninety-one. Fondly known by all as 'Mrs E', she worked for Edwards as a passenger assistant on school transport for many years, only retiring in her eighties because of cold winter weather. Always keen to keep standards high, she would read the local newspapers to check on Edwards' adverts as well as wanting to know why buses were running early or late and why windows were dirty on any local service bus that went past her home on Parish Road, Beddau.

The Covid-19 pandemic in 2020 was a tough period for Edwards, as it was for many other businesses. At the height of the pandemic, only three vehicles were in operation. Customers were reimbursed for holidays that could not operate. Edwards' 'Red Dragon' Mercedes-Benz Tourismo BF68 ZDZ participated in 'Honk for Hope' to highlight the plight of the industry and make a plea for government support. It also led a number of vehicles in a parade showing support for key NHS workers at the Royal Glamorgan Hospital. A special meeting followed on 13 July 2020 with a visit from the then Prince of Wales, who also spoke to staff that had helped residents to safety after flooding in nearby Nantgarw in February 2020. It was Prince Charles' first royal engagement since lockdown. Edwards weathered the storm and introduced various robust safety measures to ensure the safe carriage of customers and the return of the business (on 17 May 2021). Edwards won 'Best International Coach Tour Operator' at the 2021 UK Transport Awards in recognition of a strong pre-Covid-19 and bounce-back performance.

During the Go North West bus-driver strike of 2021, Edwards Coaches was one of a number of operators who provided vehicles and drivers to run local services on behalf of Go North West. Around twenty white Caetano Levantes from Edwards' National Express fleet were used on 'Orbit' services 52 and 53, 67 (Manchester to Cadishead via Salford Shopping Centre), 100 (Manchester to Warrington via Salford Shopping Centre) and 135 (Manchester to Bury via Cheetham Hill). A temporary depot was established with drivers based at the Hilton Garden Inn, exemplifying Edwards' agility.

In late 2021, Edwards borrowed Plaxton Elite-bodied Volvo B11RT X90 APP from the Oxford Bus Company for use out of the Bristol Depot as cover for a Caetano Boa Vista and for evaluation purposes on the National Express 040 service. It remained in Oxford livery with National Express stickering applied for the duration of its stay. It was new to the Oxford Bus Company in June 2016.

Four new MCV Evora-bodied Volvo B8RLE service buses arrived in 2022, entering service with a revised local livery in June. These were BV22 HCC–HCF. More new vehicles followed in 2023 in the form of Mercedes-Benz Tourismo coaches, three in touring blue and one in red for use in corporate hospitality and fitted with an evolved and multi-award-winning 'Red Dragon' livery, as well as new National Express Levante 3As.

Additional Pontypridd local services were obtained in 2024 tender wins, these leading to the purchase of the first 24-plate vehicle in the fleet, Ilesbus I-City Max RV24 FPA. Edwards was a key transport provider for the Eisteddfod, held in Pontypridd in 2024. More new tour coaches followed in the form of two PSVAR-compliant Neoplan Tourliners, OV24 VNR/S. Van Hool Y8 EDW was refurbished and received Edwards' executive livery. Ilesbus Glance RK74 ZPX and ex-Kings Ferry Irizar i8 YS17 UFJ were also acquired for executive hires. Further Mercedes-Benz Tourismos arrived, as well as a celebratory Irizar i8 for 2025.

In 2025, Edwards continues to serve as a major independent passenger-transport provider in the UK with a growing portfolio of customers and clients. Keeping to its roots, the company is proud to operate local bus services around Beddau, Llantrisant, Pontypridd and Cardiff, much as the fledgling passenger-transport business did in 1925. Exemplifying strength through diversity, the Edwards family is pleased to have grown its property portfolio and looks forward to what the future holds. The company is excited to trial electric and hydrogen vehicles, which will mark yet another milestone in the history of Edwards Coaches.

Edwards Family Tree

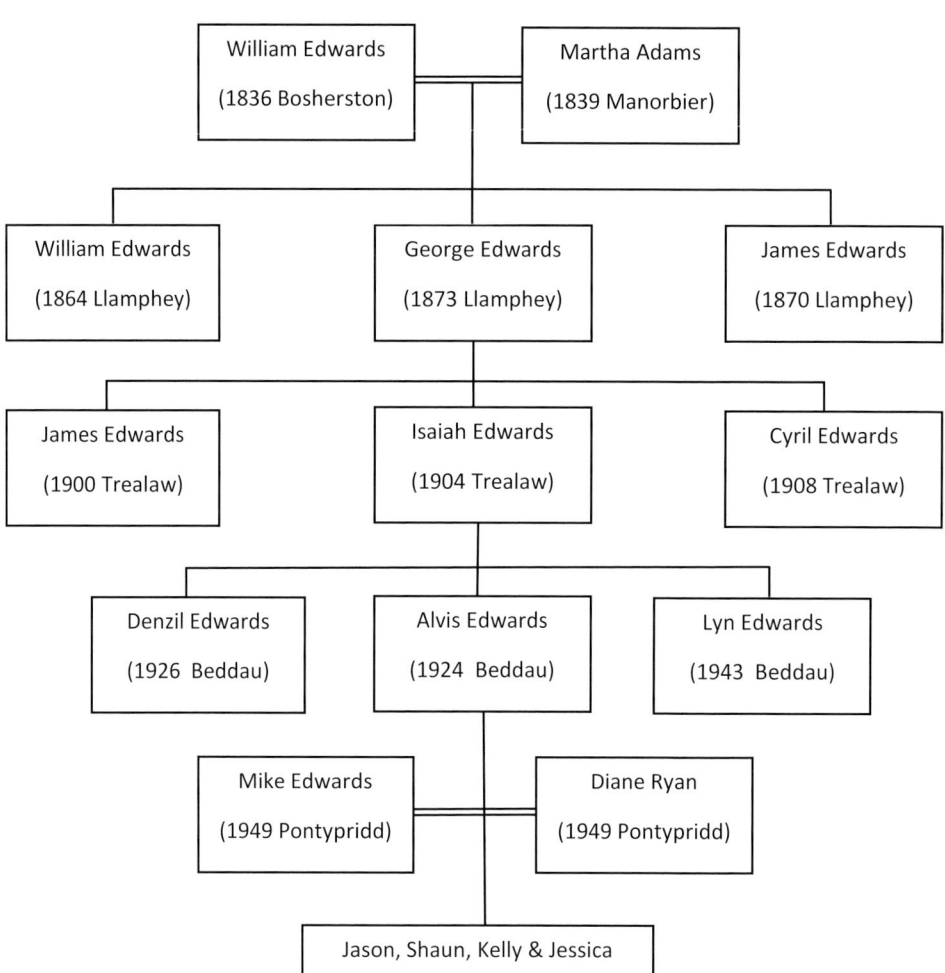

This 1920 Spa Charabanc with registration HD1393 was amongst the very first purpose-built passenger-transport vehicles purchased by Edwards. The gentleman fifth from the left with the large moustache is founder George Edwards and his youngest son, Cyril, is at the wheel. It is thought that the vehicle was new to W. James & Son Ltd with its registration mark from Dewsbury. (Edwards collection)

Amalgamated Bus Services (A.B.S.) was a joint collaboration between various local operators including Edwards to compete against Rhondda Tramways Company (Rhondda Transport Company from 1934) and South Wales Commercial Motors, later Western Welsh. James Edwards is seen at the door of Thornycroft A2 Long with a Hall Lewis twenty-seat body, registered TX 4144, entering the fleet from September 1927. (Edwards collection)

Marked 'E1' and still in the possession of Edwards, this Bundy clock key was used by Edwards for time recording in the A.B.S. days. Conductors had to 'clock in' to register their time to promote running punctually. (Edwards collection)

Star Flyer, perhaps registered UH 8279, is seen during the 1930s. Driver Isaiah Edwards is on the back row, fourth from the right. New during 1929, it would have been acquired by Edwards in June 1930 from Morse (Dealer), Cardiff. It was withdrawn during 1939 and converted to an ambulance and used in Aberdare. (Edwards collection)

From left to right, Thurgood-bodied Bedford OB GTX 911 (new to Edwards in November 1947), HNY 432 (new to Edwards in January 1948) and HTG 116 (new to Edwards in April 1948, withdrawn in 1955 and converted to a lorry) are parked alongside Duple Vista-bodied Bedford OB GTX208 (new to Edwards in October 1947) and Duple-bodied Bedford OWB FNY 70 (new in December 1942). These vehicles made up the entire Edwards fleet in January 1949. Interestingly, HTG 116 was sold to Arlington (Dealer), Cardiff, in April 1955 and became a mobile shop. (Unknown)

A variety of Edwards vehicles photographed in Beddau Square, *c.* 1949. From left to right: JNY 809, HNY 432, HTG 116, CK 3945 and GTX 208. It is claimed that CK 3945 was purchased for scrap, but examination showed the body and chassis to be in sound condition. With a year's certificate of fitness, it was decided to use it in service until it required major spending on it. Mechanically, nothing other than routine maintenance was required, so it was deemed to be a good purchase. It was withdrawn in October 1950. (Edwards collection)

Leyland TS1 with an AEC engine is seen in Sardis Road, Pontypridd, ready to make its return journey to Beddau during 1950. Mike Edwards' father, Alvis, drove the service and his mother, Jean, worked in the White Palace; Mike speculates that this is where they may have met. Its livery was thought to have been marine blue and cream, similar to that of Creamline of Neath at this time. (Alan Cross)

Burlingham-bodied Maudslay Marathon III GWP 10 was new in June 1948 to Jakeman (Regent Motorways), Redditch, and was acquired by Farley, Fochriw, in January 1951. It was acquired by Edwards in April 1953 and wore grey and red livery. It was withdrawn in November 1957 and passed to Arlington (Dealer), Cardiff, in January 1958. Records indicate that it had passed to Patterson Fruit Farms, Great Horkesley, as a staff transport vehicle by November 1960. (Roy Marshall)

A nearside shot of JNY 809 showing the 'EB' logo of Edwards Bros. Note that the sunrise painted on the radiator has five sunbeams, as opposed to the three in the next picture, and these do not fill the entire front grille. This artefact was an item of promotional material, highlighting the radio and heating apparatus included on the coach. (Edwards collection)

New to Edwards in July 1949 is JNY 809 with a Theale body, Tilling Stevens chassis and an impressive Meadows 'Big 6' engine. The vehicle is remembered as a 'cracking machine', producing a great ride with plush, luxury seating. It was later repainted in the grey and red livery and was eventually sold to Bebb for spares in February 1958. Alvis Edwards is seen driving this, his regular coach, past the Odeon in Leicester Square, London, during the 1950s. He received a fine for an 'unrecordable speed' in Oxfordshire with this motor! (Edwards collection)

The Public Service Vehicle driver badge belonging to Alvis Edwards, GG11668. Alvis was the father of Mike Edwards, son of Isaiah and grandson of George Edwards. The letters 'GG' denote the South Wales Traffic Commissioners' area. (Edwards collection)

Burlingham-bodied Maudslay Marathon III HAB 905 arrived with Edwards from Stephens, Tredegar, in May 1957 and wore Edwards' grey and red livery. It was new to Hayes of Lye, Worcestershire, in March 1949. It passed to Arlington (Dealer), Cardiff, in late 1960 before passing to Robins, Mountain Ash, by December 1960. (Roy Marshall)

Burlingham-bodied AEC Regal III JTX 667 was new to Edwards in February 1950. It was withdrawn in November 1958 and passed to Reliance Motor Services, Newbury, via Arlington (Dealer), Cardiff. It is seen with 'Tour' on its destination blind, denoting its purpose on the day that the photograph was taken in the early 1950s. (Unknown)

Duple Vega-bodied Bedford SB LNY 586 was new to Edwards in 1951 and passed to Arlington (Dealer) Cardiff, in May 1956 before passing to Williams, Pumpsaint (Carmarthenshire). Notice the Edwards crest on the offside centre. It is pictured in London in the early 1950s. (Edwards collection)

Gwyneth Edwards, Mike Edwards' grandmother, in front of JTX 667 when new in 1950. (Edwards collection)

Mike and his mother, Jean Edwards, are seen outside 46 Danygraig Street, *c.* 1954. The vehicle is Burlingham-bodied AEC Regal III JTX 667. (Edwards collection)

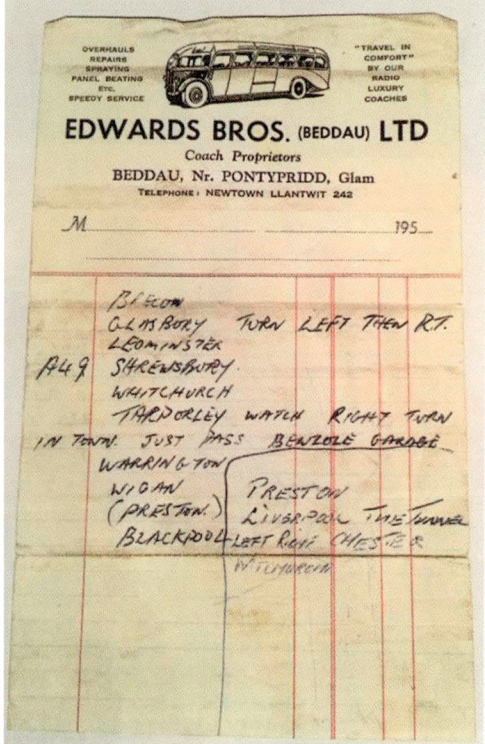

An Edwards work ticket from the 1950s, given to Mike Edwards by the grandson of former driver Charlie Hutchins as a memento from the decade. Note the wording on the top right of the paper, 'travel in comfort by our radio luxury coaches', and the garage services available from Edwards at the top left. The directional instructions appear rudimentary compared with what is required for the complex nature of roads today. (Edwards collection)

Burlingham Seagull-bodied Bedford SBG RTX 246 was new to Edwards in mid-1955, purchased from Arlington (Dealer), Cardiff. The vehicle was cream and red when new, though grey replaced the cream, in keeping with Edwards colours, after several months. It was sold back to Arlington in October 1964, when it was based at their Blackweir premises for several weeks. It is seen on Sardis Road during the 1950s. (Unknown)

Bedford SB3 Duple Vega XNY 370 was new in December 1957. It was withdrawn in January 1968 and appeared at Morris Bros, Swansea, one month later. It is pictured in the early to mid-1960s alongside Western Welsh Leyland Tiger Cub UKG 268 with fleet number 1268 on the 240 service to Porthcawl in the turning area behind Pontypridd Station, with the Graig in the background. (Roy Marshall)

Entitled 'Football Fixtures' but also including Rugby for 1960/61, this leaflet features an advert for 'Coach Proprietors' Edwards. Services listed are overhauls, repairs, spraying and panel beating, etc. at a speedy service. Persuasion to entice potential customers, it also states 'travel in comfort by our radio luxury coaches'. (Edwards collection)

In the early 1960s, Duple Midland-bodied Bedford SB8 741 ENY is seen on Sardis Road, Pontypridd, with the now demolished cinema in the background. It was new to Edwards in June 1960 and was sold to Arlington (Dealer), Cardiff, in late 1966. It is thought that the vehicle was then exported to Ireland in 1968. (A. J. Douglas)

New to Davies, Pencader, in February/March 1957 is Duple Midland-bodied Bedford SBO OBX 100. It was acquired by Edwards in July 1960 and passed to Arlington (Dealer), Cardiff, in July 1967. It was sold to Sing, Cardiff, in August 1967 and is reported to have passed to Osmonds, Curry Rivel, by November 1967. It is thought that this photograph was taken in Edwards' premises in the mid-1960s. (Unknown)

Duple Super Vega-bodied Bedford SB8 was photographed in the parking area behind Pontypridd railway station in the mid-1960s. It was new in January 1961 and was acquired from Demery, Morriston, around January 1963, retaining Demery's orange and beige livery which was adopted for future intakes. Other vehicles similarly repainted at this time were 141 ENY, OBX 100, XNY 370 and 405 MTG. YCY 790 was withdrawn in November 1967. (Roy Marshall)

Burlingham Seagull-bodied Bedford SBG SWW 659 was new to Wilkinson, Silsden, in October 1956, passing to Edwards via Humphries, Bridgend, in September 1968. It is seen in the parking area behind Pontypridd Station at some point between 1968 and January 1970, when it left the fleet and passed to Everall, Wolverhampton. (Roy Marshall)

One of six new to Worthington, Birmingham, in March 1956, Duple Corinthian-bodied Commer Avenger III TOA 285 had a short life with Edwards. It was acquired in June 1968 from Richards Bros, Moylgrove, and was withdrawn in October of the same year. (Edwards collection)

Duple Super Vega-bodied Bedford SB1 WGD 566 is seen outside the post office on Broadway, Pontypridd, *c.* 1968. This is now the site of a Wetherspoons pub named The Tumble Inn, taking its name from the area known as 'the tumble' by locals after horse-drawn tubs or drams were emptied of coal by tumbling them over as they journeyed to and from the pits in Victorian times. This bus was new to McIntyre, Newton Mearns, in 1959 and acquired by Edwards from Jenkins, Skewen, in June 1967. It passed to Arlington (Dealer), Cardiff, in September 1969. (Unknown)

Bedford VAM14 MCW PTG 242F, new in November 1967, is seen on Wood Street, Cardiff, on 23 March 1969. The vehicle is thought to have been scrapped by October 1979 after passing through the owners of York, Chorlton-cum-Hardy (1971), Morris, Bromyard (1974), and Cave, Shirley (1978). (Mike Street)

Photographed on 4 April 1972 in the Beddau Garage is CNY 619J, Plaxton Panorama Elite II-bodied Seddon Pennine 4. It was new to Edwards in January 1971, passed to Moseley, Cinderford, in February 1973 and was then reacquired by Edwards in June 1974. (John Jones)

Duple Viceroy-bodied Bedford YRQ ENY 771J was new to Edwards in July 1971. It is seen on 4 June 1972 at Edwards Garage (on the corner of Gwaunmiskin Road and Tynant Road, Beddau). It passed to Moseley (Dealer), Cinderford, in February 1973 and then Ring Road, Bradford, in May 1973. (John Jones)

Photographed on 4 June 1972 is Duple Viceroy-bodied Bedford VAM70. It was new to Edwards in August 1969. It passed to Moseley (Dealer), Cinderford, in May 1972 and then Bexleyheath Transport in October 1972. (John Jones)

Photographed in Salt Lake Car Park, Porthcawl, on 25 June 1972 is Plaxton Panorama Elite II-bodied Seddon Pennine 4 CNY 618J. It was new to Edwards in February 1971 and passed via Wilson (Carnwath) Reed (Guildford), Carnell (Sutton Bridge) and Short (Wingland) before being scrapped around May 1993. (Mike Street)

Weymann-bodied Leyland Tiger Cub KDB 655 is seen in Beddau on 27 February 1973. It was new to North Western with fleet number 655 in March 1956 and passed to Edwards via Hills of Tredegar. (John Jones)

Photographed at Beddau Garage on 27 February 1973 is Duple Super Vega-bodied Bedford SB1 WCE 528. It was new in May 1960 to Harris, Cambridge, and passed to Edwards from Berkeley Coaches, Paulton, in September 1970. It was sold in July 1974. (John Jones)

Plaxton Panorama IV-bodied Bedford SB5 MTX 945L is photographed at Salt Lake Car Park, Porthcawl, on 23 June 1974. It was new to Edwards in March 1973. Later in its life, it is thought to have been converted into a mobile home. (Mike Street)

Pictured at Salt Lake Car Park, Porthcawl, on 23 June 1974 is Plaxton Panorama Elite III-bodied AEC Reliance MTX 949L, new to Edwards in February 1973. It left for Bruce & Parker, Okehampton, in December 1974 before passing to other operators. (Mike Street)

Seddon Pennine 6 Duple Dominant NTG 9L is seen in Salt Lake Car Park, Porthcawl, on 23 June 1974. It had been new to Bebb in April 1973. It would later pass to other operators including one of the same name, Edwards of Joys Green, in December 1975. It is thought to have been exported during May 1985. (Mike Street)

Another photograph from June 1974 at Salt Lake Car Park, Porthcawl, features Duple Vega 31-bodied Bedford SB5 GTX 547K. It was new to Edwards in March 1972, later passing to Thomas of Gorseinon (September 1975) via Bebb (August 1975). Being sold to Moseley (Dealer) in March 1977, it passed to Massey, Market Weighton, for non-PSV use. It was scrapped around 1985. Mike Edwards recalls driving this coach to Deventer, Holland, transporting a Football team from Rumney, Cardiff. It was the first of two SB5s new to Edwards in 1972. (Mike Street)

In a snowy scene from the 1980s, Duple Viceroy-bodied Bedford YRT is seen with drivers Duncan Powell and Bob Powell. It was acquired by Edwards from Lothian Regional Transport around September 1982, and was new ten years prior to this. (Edwards collection)

Duple Dominant II-bodied Ford R1114 was new to Whittle, Highley, in February 1980 when it was thought to have held the unusual fleet number of 0. It passed to Edwards via Bebb at the start of 1987 and was withdrawn in July 2000. It is seen in the Llantwit Fardre Depot in the late 1980s. (Edwards collection)

Plaxton Supreme IV-bodied Volvo B58-56 GHB 197V is photographed in the Llantwit Fardre Depot during the 1980s. It was new as BWN 811V to West Wales, Tycroes, in October 1979, passing to D Coaches, Morriston, in September 1984. It was acquired by Edwards in April 1986 and re-registered 978 HHT in July 1987. In May 1988, it reverted to its original registration and transferred to Letherby, Trebanog, later to be re-acquired by Edwards (January 1989). It became 219 LUO in October 1992, later passing to Glyncoch Swingers Jazz Band. (Edwards collection)

Duple Dominant I-bodied Ford R1114 WNP 861R was new in July 1977 to Halford, Kempsey, and is pictured in the Llantwit Fardre Depot during the 1980s. It passed to Bebb around 1987 and was scrapped during 1992. (Edwards collection)

XDW 602K is seen at Edwards' Beddau Garage on 23 January 1983. It is a Duple Viceroy-bodied Ford R226, new in March 1972 to Dolan's (Shamrock) Coaches of Newport, passing to Edwards via Miles, Gelligaer, during 1982. (John Jones)

With Edwards of Beddau fleet names, Caetano Estoril II-bodied Ford R1114 TTX 32S is pictured at Edwards' Beddau Garage on 8 July 1984. It was new to Bebb in June 1978. (John Jones)

Incorporating; Mayfayre Coaches & Galvin Tours

EDWARDS TRAVEL

**20 - 53 SEATER COACHES FOR CONTRACT & PRIVATE HIRE
TOURS & EXCURSIONS**

Reg. Office;
**Atlantic Industrial Est
Llantwit Fardre,
Pontypridd**

Tel; (0443) 206379
**After Hours
202642 or 203843**

A business card from around 1985. Note 'Incorporating Mayfayre Coaches & Galvin Tours' and the address of 'Atlantic Industrial Est'. (Edwards collection)

New in June 1967 to World Wide Coaches Limited, Camberwell, Plaxton Panorama I-bodied AEC Reliance UNK 616E is pictured in Edwards' Llantwit Fardre Depot, *c.* 1985. It was acquired in 1984 from South Glamorgan County Council where it was used by Barry Youth Club, making a few trips to Lake Balaton in the Czech Republic before acquisition by Edwards. It passed to Glyncoch Swingers Jazz Band around 1986. Also visible is a Duple Viceroy-bodied Ford R226, XDW 602K, alongside the vehicle inspection ramp. (Edwards collection)

Photographed on 17 June 1986 at the Llantwit Fardre Depot is Duple Dominant-bodied Leyland Leopard NNW 122P with 'Galvin Tours' on the nearside. It was new ten years previous in April 1976 to Wallace Arnold. It was withdrawn in September 1988 with accident damage. (Edwards collection)

New to Newport Transport in April 1971 is Alexander J-bodied Leyland Atlantean PDR1A/1 TDW 315J. It is photographed in Edwards' Llantwit Fardre Depot in the livery of its former owner, Taff Ely, not long after acquisition in April 1987. Note the green paint from its former Newport life evident at the front. Edwards built up a sizable and varied fleet of double-deck buses for use on school contracts, operating these successfully alongside the coach fleet for many years. (Edwards collection)

Caetano Estoril II-bodied Ford R1114 was new to Bebb in September 1978, passing to Edwards via Clough, Pontypridd, during April 1986. It was scrapped in April 1994. It is photographed at the Llantwit Fardre Depot during the late 1980s. (Edwards collection)

Plaxton Paramount 3500 C262 GUH was new to National Welsh with a Leyland Tiger engine and fleet code XC262 in March 1986. It entered the Edwards fleet in the early 1990s, around the time when this photograph was taken. It was purchased from Edwards for preservation in 2015 and is restored in National Express livery and has attended various running days and transport events. At some point in its history, its original Leyland Tiger engine was replaced with a Volvo B10M unit. (Edwards collection)

Photographed outside the National Museum of Wales, Cardiff, on 28 September 1990 is Leyland PSU5C/4R Plaxton Supreme V SND 295X, which was new to National Travel (West) in November 1981. Edwards acquired this vehicle in September 1989; it remained in the fleet until the early 2000s. (Mike Street)

New to Greater Manchester PTE in January 1975, Leyland Atlantean AN68/1R GDB 174N is photographed leaving the Llantwit Fardre Depot on 17 May 1991. It previously also worked for East Kent. A model produced by EFE is available of similar GDB 168N in London Country South West livery. (Edwards collection)

Leyland Atlantean PDR2/1 with Alexander J bodywork WTN 647H is photographed in Llantwit Fardre Depot in the early 1990s. It was new to Tyne & Wear PTE in February 1970, later passing to Rennies of Dunfermline, remnants of its time there evident in the topmost destination panel. It passed to Edwards via Mainwaring (Mainline Travel), Tonyrefail, in August 1984. Fleet number 47 is painted above the 'E' logo on the front. Fleet numbers have generally not been used on Edwards vehicles, with vehicles instead more commonly referred to by registration plate, in part or full. (Edwards collection)

Alexander A-bodied Leyland Atlantean PDR1/1 MUS 281F is seen exiting the Llantwit Fardre Depot on 17 May 1991. It was new to Glasgow Corporation Transport in May 1967 and came to reside with the Glasgow Vintage Vehicle Trust with its original registration KUS 607E. It attended the 'Leyland Atlantean 40' event at the Historic Commercial Vehicle Museum, Leyland, in September 1998, celebrating the anniversary of the first Leyland Atlantean produced. (Edwards collection)

Leyland Atlantean PDR1A/1 with Alexander J bodywork PAG 760H was new to 'A1 Service' Member Tom Hunter of Crosshouse, Ayrshire. It was one of a number of buses damaged in an arson attack at his premises in 1978. It was repaired and passed to Gilchrist of East Kilbride, George Paterson of Hamilton and Rennies of Dunfermline before sale to Edwards in May 1986. It is seen in the Llantwit Fardre Depot on 17 May 1991. (Edwards collection)

Photographed leaving the Llantwit Fardre Depot on 17 May 1991 is 978 HHT, an AEC Reliance with Plaxton Elite bodywork but with Supreme front mouldings. It was new to Smith, Wigan, in April 1969 as GEK 801G and was acquired by Edwards from Evans, Church Village, in January 1987. It received registration 978 HHT in May 1988. It was re-registered to UAX 71G in December 1991, just before withdrawal. (Edwards collection)

DAF MB200 with Plaxton Paramount 3200 bodywork A546 XUH is photographed in the Llantwit Fardre Depot in the early 1990s. It was new to Letherby, Trebanog, in April 1984, passing to Edwards from that source in May 1988 and wore registration 978 HHT from December 1991 until early 2007, when it was withdrawn. (Edwards collection)

A newspaper cutting from 1993 details the closure of Humphreys Coaches and how Edwards stepped in to fill the void. To the right of the article, a brief history of Edwards is provided. A number of authorised booking agents are also included with Alvis Edwards and various others listed. Pictured are Alan Clough, Mike Edwards and Keith Marsham. (Cardiff Transport Preservation Group archive)

ECW-bodied Bristol VRT GTX 756W was new to National Welsh in October 1980. It was damaged in the Barry Depot fire of 22 August 1986 but a Leyland Olympian alongside was completely destroyed. It was repaired and reinstated in September 1986, entering the Edwards fleet in August 1992 from Rhondda Buses. It is photographed in the Llantwit Fardre Depot alongside various Leyland Atlanteans during the mid-1990s. It was de-roofed in an accident at Cross Inn in June 1997 and left the Edwards fleet but served elsewhere as an open-top until scrapped in 2011. (Ken Mumford)

A line-up of school vehicles in the Llantwit Fardre Depot in the mid-1990s. Closest is Alexander L-bodied Leyland Atlantean PDR2/1, new to Merseyside PTE as XKC 816K in September 1971. It made its way to the Isle of Man and registered V649 MAN before being repatriated and given registration BPA 342K. It was acquired by Edwards in September 1994 from Thomas, West Ewell, later receiving school-bus yellow with its centre door panelled over. It was scrapped around 2005. Alongside is Roe-bodied Leyland Atlantean AN68/1R TRT 95M and Alexander J-bodied Leyland Atlantean PDR1A/1 PAG 760H. (Ken Mumford)

Photographed on a private hire in Porthcawl in the mid-1990s is Plaxton Paramount-bodied DAF MB230 E321 TTX. It was new to Humphreys of Pontypridd in April 1988 and entered the Edwards fleet in October 1993 as Edwards stepped in to fill the void that would be left by the closure of Humphreys Coaches. It was the last vehicle purchased by Humphreys and its last trip prior to passing to Edwards was a tour of Scarborough. (Peter Owen)

Photographed on Westgate Street, Cardiff, on 4 May 1995 is LPP 347V, a Ford R1114 Duple Dominant new to Dickson, Stoke Mandeville, in January 1980. Having operated with Thomas, Tonypandy, after Mott, Stoke Mandeville, it made its way to the Edwards fleet in April 1990. During 1993, it received a Ford Cargo engine and was used for around another three years before withdrawal. (Mike Street)

AEC Reliance with Plaxton Supreme III bodywork MUH 949P was new to Humphreys, Pontypridd, in July 1976 and was later acquired by Edwards. It had the reputation of being the fastest in the Humphreys fleet. It is seen heading to the Bus and Coach Wales rally being held on the site of the former Woodham Brothers Scrapyard at Barry Island on 21 May 1995. It was scrapped in 1996. (John Jones)

Carrying Alexander J bodywork, Leyland Atlantean PDR1A/1 ULJ 252J is photographed leaving the Llantwit Fardre Depot to commence a school run on 5 July 1995. It was new to Bournemouth Corporation in January 1971 and entered the Edwards fleet from Cyril Evans, Senghenydd, in October 1990. (Stephen Vallance collection)

Duple Dominant II-bodied Ford R1014 NRO 266V was new to Ralphs, Longford, in July 1980. It was acquired by Edwards in September 1995 with Gibson and Gray, Pontypridd, having previously operated with Watts, Bonvilston. It is thought to have had its chassis shortened by Tricentrol and is seen on a wholly supported Talbot Green local service, number 47, in the mid to late 1990s. It was withdrawn by Edwards in November 2004 and scrapped soon after. (Simon Nicholas)

Metro Cammell Weymann-bodied Leyland PD2/40 FRJ 243D was new to Salford Corporation in April 1966. *Bus and Coach Preservation* magazine published an extensive article on this vehicle in June 1998, at that time thought to be Britain's only half-cab Leyland in regular service all year round. It is seen at the Bus and Coach Wales Rally at Barry Island on 2 June 1996, painted in colours reminiscent of Edwards' 1925 livery. It later passed to a confectionery business in Bungay, Suffolk, which turned it into a mobile 'Only Fools and Horses' museum. (Mike Street)

An artist's impression of what the grey and red Edwards livery might look like on a modern double-decker, an Alexander Dennis Enviro 400MMC. None of these have entered the fleet to date, its registration YX24 EDW making reference to its fictitious ownership. (Digital impression by Andrew Cairns)

New to South Wales' Brunswick garage in May 1982 and registered MCY 114X, Leyland Leopard Duple Dominant IV MKH 730A is photographed at the Bus and Coach Wales Rally at Barry Island on 2 June 1996. It made its way to Edwards in September 1994, passing via United Welsh and Brewers. It would later pass to Hemmings Travel, Blaengarw, and Movereturn, Pontycymmer, before withdrawal in 1992. (Mike Street)

Bova Futura FHD12-340 R630VYB was one of a pair new to Edwards in September 1997 and is seen in the Llantwit Fardre Depot when nearly new. It would become LUI 7923 in November 2003 at the same time as sister vehicle R631 VYB became NUI 3217. (Edwards collection)

DAF MB200 Jonckheere Jubilee P50 YAP 104 was new to Roman City, Bath, in April 1985 with registration B495 CBD. Edwards acquired the vehicle in December 1986 and ran it in the colours of Roman City with the 'Edwards Travel' fleet name for a period of time. It would be registered YAP 104 in March 1991. It is seen at Jamaica Inn on 3 October 1997. It lasted in the fleet until withdrawal in 2008, the cherished registration remaining like many others. (Mike Street)

Roe-bodied Leyland Atlantean AN68/1R TRT 95M is seen in the Llantwit Fardre Depot on 4 October 1998, this time wearing its cream Edwards livery. Note the logo on the front and side which depicts 'The Old Bridge' (or 'Yr Hen Bont') in Pontypridd. It was built in 1756 by William Edwards, a self-taught stonemason, though there are no links to the Edwards Coaches family. This wasn't the only depiction of the bridge used on Edwards vehicles but was one of the most prominent applications, applied by painter Jeff. (Andy Baldwin)

Still in the livery of its previous owner Phil Anslow Travel, Leyland Atlantean AN68A/1R with East Lancs bodywork LFR 129T is seen on a school run in Pontypridd, *c.* 1999. It was new to Blackburn Transport in July 1979 and during most of its time there wore a commemorative livery to celebrate fifty years of buses in the town. It was later in the fleet of Howells Coaches, Deri, until being scrapped in 2013. (Unknown)

East Lancs-bodied Leyland Atlantean AN68A/1R STD 197L is photographed in Tonteg on 9 June 1999. It was new to Fishwick, Leyland, in October 1972 and passed to Edwards via Rennies, Dunfermline, and later operated for Howells of Deri. (John Jones)

Photographed in Alpe d'Huez, French Alps, in the late 1990s is Bova Futura FHD12-340 M542 JHB. In April 2001, it was re-registered to SIL 5382. Prior to withdrawal, it was used in the school transport fleet, first in yellow and then later in the blue colour scheme. (Stephen Griffin)

Duple Laser-bodied Bedford YNT B221 OJU is photographed travelling through Llantwit Fardre on 13 July 2000. New to Bexleyheath Transport in April 1985, it passed to Edwards with Gibson and Gray, Pontypridd, in September 1995. It went to a scrap dealer in Cardiff for disposal in June 2004. (John Jones)

Photographed in Church Village on 17 July 2000 is Park Royal-bodied Leyland Atlantean AN68A/1R NRN 397P. It was new to Ribble in April 1976, holding fleet number 1397, passing to Edwards via Finglands, Greater Manchester (where it held fleet number 1735), in April 1997. It is now preserved, fully restored in Ribble National Bus Company livery. (John Jones)

Edwards drivers Stuart Russell, Steve Warren, Gavin James, Terry Burke, Mark Cooper and Darren Williams stand in front of Edwards' new Scania Irizar Century vehicles, registered Y36–38HHE, which were new in March 2001. (Edwards collection)

Photographed in Upper Boat on 21 May 2001 and being followed by a Volvo Ailsa B55-10 is East Lancs-bodied Leyland Atlantean AN68/1R BTV 651T. It was new to Nottingham City Transport in February 1979 with fleet number 651, passing to Edwards via Blue Bird of Neath. It had been withdrawn by November 2004. (John Jones)

Bova Europa AEF32Y is photographed in Upper Boat on 21 May 2001. It was new to United in June 1983 and wore National Holidays and National Express livery during its time there. It entered the Edwards fleet from Gray's, Pontypridd, in September 1995. It was sent to T&H Commercials, Brynmawr, in 2005 for scrap. (John Jones)

Duple Caribbean I-bodied DAF MB200 A228 LRU is captured in Tynant on 21 May 2001. It was new in May 1984 to Cled Williams, Bargoed, passing to Edwards in August 1997 and was scrapped during 2007. (John Jones)

Coach and bus operation seeks buyer

SOUTH WALES coach and bus operator, Atlantic Transport Services, trading as Edwards Coaches is looking for a buyer.

It has been advertised for by Simon Girling of Grant Thornton, Bristol, acting on behalf of court-appointed receiver David Thomas.

Partners Peter Ryan and Mike Edwards continue to run the business but applied to the court to appoint a receiver who could effect the sale.

Edwards has been established 20 years and has a fleet

Business as usual while Edwards business is up for sale

of 65 vehicles, which are operated from a two-acre freehold site.

It generated £3.5 million turnover - £1.5 million from contracts and private hire, £2

million from coach holidays. David Thomas is acting as court-appointed receiver in accordance with the terms of the Court Order dated 18 August 2000.

Mike Edwards buys out his partner's share

EDWARDS Coaches of Llantwit Fardre has been bought out by Mike Edwards, one of the partners in the business. Although the business has been in the Edwards family for 75 years it was taken over by Mike Edwards and brother-in-law Peter Ryan in 1977.

Edwards Coaches is pleased that the period of uncertainty over its future has been ended. Speculation over a possible takeover had led to staff leaving their bookings elsewhere. Mike Edwards and tour manager Alan Clough now look forward to bringing the company back on track and planning for future development.

Articles from August and October 2000 detailing the transition of Edwards Coaches into the hands of Mike Edwards. (Cardiff Transport Preservation Group archive)

Bova Futura FHD12-370 CN51 SVR is seen on a tour to Babbacombe in the early 2000s. From August 2013, it would receive the cherished registration K600 EDW. It was one of three new to Edwards in September 2001, the others being CN51 SUF and CN51 SXB, which received registrations K700 EDW and K444 EDW, respectively, also in August 2013. (Unknown)

Ex-Cardiff Bus Northern Counties-bodied Volvo Ailsa B55-10 A428 VNY is seen alongside Scania Irizar Century Y37HHE at the Cardiff Centenary rally in the city of Cardiff in 2002. Approximately thirty Volvo Ailsa B55-10s operated with Edwards, the majority from Cardiff Bus. (Peter Owen)

Former West Midlands Travel MK1 MCW Metrobus GOG 125W is photographed on a private hire opposite Cardiff Castle during the mid-2000s. It was new in November 1980 and passed to Edwards via McColl's of Balloch during 2002. It was scrapped in 2007 and was one of eighteen MCW Metrobuses to have operated with Edwards. (Richard Field)

Ex-Cardiff Bus Northern Counties-bodied Volvo Ailsa B55-10 NDW 416X is seen resting in Cardiff city centre in the mid-2000s. Note the graphic on the lower rear window advertising Edwards holidays as well as between the decks on the offside alongside the 'school bus' vinyl. It was scrapped in 2007. Sister vehicles NDW 408X and NDW 409X from the same source were the only ones latterly repainted into Edwards' blue livery. (Peter Owen)

In this newspaper advert from around 2002 Edwards encourages potential clients to 'Put your feet up and travel in style'. It featured two Bovas as front-line coaches of the time. Note that 'some coaches offer air conditioning', whereas this comes as standard today. (Cardiff Transport Preservation Group archive)

A tri-axle Bova Futura FHD14-430 CN04 XCC outside the Thistle Hotel in Manchester during the mid to late 2000s. As tri-axles were less common then, the vehicle was deemed to be the bane of the drivers' and Edwards' lives. Numerous tail-swing incidents occurred which required the replacement of lower engine covers (thanks to Gordon Tucker's creativity with fibreglass) and panelling. (Mark Cooper)

Plaxton Paramount 3200-bodied Volvo B10M-60 K600 BUL was new to Bullock, Cheadle, as K433 ANE in March 1993. It was acquired by Edwards during 2002 and lasted in the fleet until 2016. It was photographed in the mid-2000s in the Llantwit Fardre Depot. During its time at Edwards, it also wore registration PIL 2598. (Richard Field)

Seventy-seat Marcopolo Viaggio II-bodied MAN 18.310 CN54 LGE was one of four new to Edwards between September and November 2004, the others being CN54 GFV, CN54 GFX and CN54 LGF. These were bought to modernise Edwards' school bus fleet and to offer high-capacity vehicles to schools interested in vehicle hire for longer journeys. CN54 LGE and a sister vehicle are photographed outside Cardiff Castle in the mid-2000s. (Richard Field)

Mike Edwards and Alastair Wilson of Evobus with the three new Setra S415HDs, BX04 NBE, BX04 NBG and BX04 NBF, in the Llantwit Fardre Depot shortly after delivery. Note the seventy-five years of service emblem above the nearside wheel. (Edwards collection)

Photographed outside the Vale of Glamorgan Hotel, Golf and Country Club in the mid-2000s is Setra S415HD BX04 NBE and an unidentified white Bova behind. (Edwards collection)

Later registered 978HHT, Setra S415HD BX04 NBG is seen at a transport event in the mid-2000s promoting the Edwards suite of tours, including 'Turkey and Tinsel', 'Ireland' and 'Jersey', the latter available from just £219. (Peter Owen)

EDWARDS' SETRAS TAKEN FOR TOURS

SOUTH Wales operator Edward's Coaches has snapped up the last four Setra 315 GT HDs to come off the manufacturer's Ulm production line.

Owner Mike Edwards heard production was ending and moved quickly to get his order in: Edwards' customers like the wide entrance and grab rails. Edwards caters for many different types of customer on its 75-strong fleet, including over 50 yellow school buses, but his core market on the executive side of the business are over 55 holidaymakers.

Consequently, the vehicles are highly specified: air con, fridge, hot drinks and DVD amongst other refinements. But the feature Edwards is most proud of is the top-of-the-range reclining Ambiente seats: "our customers think they are fabulous," he says and they must too since holidays are up 30% on 2004.

It has been a really good year for Edwards so far: business is good, the firm is celebrating its 80th year

and one of the new Setras won two awards, best Welsh Coach and the Boon Cup for Best Co-ordinated Design, at the UK Coach Rally in Brighton. But Mike does not take the credit for the latter – he took his wife with him when he went to the factory to make his order. The stunning blue colour scheme is down to her.

Edwards prefer 49 seat executive coaches because it fits in with their booking software, and means that if there is ever a problem the company can make a quick substitution and the customers will never know the difference. He likes to keep his coaches for between 7 to 10 years and reckons Setras are capable of lasting the distance, he also runs a

couple of 415 deckers, one of which is currently in use by the Welsh International Rugby team.

Edwards will not say what he paid for fear of upsetting Alistair Wilson at EvoBus, the supplier, but did say, "we got a very good deal."

FACT FILE

Fact file:	
Chassis/ engine:	Setra/ 315 GT HD
Body:	
Transmission:	AS-Tronic
Seats:	49
Spec:	'Ambiente' seats, air con, fridge, hot drinks, DVD

An article from *Coach and Bus Week* from July 2005 detailing Edwards' acquisition of some of the last Setra 315 GT-HDs to come off the production line. These were registered BX05 UVR, BX05 UVS, BX05 UVT and BX05 UVU. (Cardiff Transport Preservation Group archive)

Setra 315 GT-HD BX05 UVS photographed in Abergavenny on a market day, *c.* 2006. It would receive registration P300 EDW in June 2013, the same time that sister vehicles in the batch received P200, P400 and P500 EDW. (Edwards collection)

Alexander RV-bodied Volvo Ailsa B55-10 DEM 822Y was new to Merseybus PTE in 1982 as one of two vehicles acquired by them for evaluation purposes. It and sister vehicle DEM 821Y also operated for Cardiff Bus before being acquired by Edwards as school buses. It became common practice for Edwards to blank off the upper front and rear windows in the interests of limiting anti-social behaviour. DEM 822Y is seen at the Barry Festival of Transport in June 2008 alongside Setra S416GT-HD BK08 NJU. (Peter Owen)

Marshall Master-bodied Mercedes-Benz Vario O810D S637 MGA is seen in Pontypridd on contracted service 18 to Ty Rhiw in June 2008. It would be just short of another two years before Edwards started up their own commercial local services. (Peter Owen)

Alexander Dash-bodied Dennis Dart N25 OBO is seen on North Road, Cardiff, in yellow school-transport livery on 24 September 2008. It was new to Cardiff Bus with fleet number 025 in 1995, lasting in the Edwards fleet until withdrawal in July 2013. (G. L. Phillips)

Setra S415HD BX04 NBG is seen at Blackwood Bus Station on 10 January 2009. By this time it had become the official Welsh Rugby Team coach, appropriately adorned with WRU decals. (G. L. Phillips)

Wearing its flag livery, Bova Futura FHD13.340XE WA06 JFZ is photographed outside the Hilton London Metropole Hotel in the mid to late 2000s. It received registration XBZ 4111 in December 2013. It was one of two new to Edwards in March 2006, the other being WA06 JFY. (Mark Cooper)

On 13 July 2009, Bova Magiq XHD122.340XE WA06 JFX is photographed alongside MS *Prinsendam* at the Port of Newport as part of its twelve-day cruise around the UK and Ireland. Edwards assisted in transferring mainly American guests on excursions to Cardiff, Newport (the host city to the Ryder Cup the following year) and Bath. It was later registered NXI 813. (Edwards collection)

Setra S416GT-HD BX07 NMO, which would later become L700 EDW, is photographed after snowfall in Zell am See, Austria, in 2009. (Edwards collection)

DAF MB200 Plaxton Paramount 3200 RIL 1759 was new to Humphreys of Pontypridd in 1986 as C598 HTX and entered the Edwards fleet in 1993 following the closure of Humphreys. It is seen on a school duty in Pontypridd during May 2010, at this point being twenty-four years old, again demonstrating the longevity that can be achieved through attentive maintenance practices. (Peter Owen)

A poster advertising Edwards' return to local bus services. It promotes providing a better service than that offered in the area at the time by the incumbent operator, Veolia Transport Cymru, by offering low-floor and clean vehicles, a punctual service and friendly ex-Bebb drivers! (Alexander Jeenes)

Wright Crusader-bodied Dennis Dart SLF LAZ7641 was acquired by Edwards in March 2010 when it was re-entering local bus-service work. It is seen in the Llantwit Fardre Depot soon after arrival, prior to receiving Edwards' blue livery. It was new in February 1997 to Belfast Citybus with fleet number 641 and used on the free shuttle service to and from the Gas Works. Seven others were also acquired from the same source, these being DCZ 7649, DCZ 7650, YAZ 8643, YAZ 8644, YAZ 8645, YAZ 8646 and YAZ 8647. (Mike Davies)

New to Cardiff Bus in October 1997, passing with the rest of the batch to Reading Buses but acquired by Edwards from Invincible, Tamworth, during April 1010 is Optare Excel R209 DKG. It is photographed outside the Hollybush in Church Village on 16 June 2010 – the site where a Bundy clock was formerly located. It was the only one of the type to have been operated by Edwards, lasting in the fleet until 2016. (John Jones)

Alexander Dash-bodied Dennis Dart N28 OBO is photographed on Greyfriars Road, Cardiff, on the 400 service during 2010. It was new to Cardiff Bus in December 1995 with fleet number 028. It was acquired by Edwards in September 2008 with N25 OBO and initially wore yellow school-bus livery. Unlike N25 OBO, it later received Edwards' blue livery. (Peter Owen)

Adorned with balloons, Setra S416GT-HD BK08 NJU is spotted inside the Edwards Depot on an open day in January 2010. *Hi-de-Hi!* star Ruth Madoc attended as a guest. Vinyl on its bumper denotes that this vehicle was winner of 'Coach of the Year' at the 2008 UK Coach Rally. (Peter Owen)

New to Speedlink Airport Services in 1993, Plaxton Premiere 350 Volvo B10M K200 SAS is photographed in Llantwit Fardre Depot in January 2011. Later registered SOI 196, it entered the Edwards fleet from Wilkins of Cymmer, as evident by its adapted livery. It previously wore National Express livery as a result of their acquisition of Speedlink. (Peter Owen)

Wright Crusader Dennis Dart SLF DCZ 7650 is seen in Talbot Green working the 100E service to Pontypridd on 23 April 2011. It passed to Lloyds Coaches, Machynlleth, in November 2011. (Tudor Thomas)

Wrightbus Streetlite WF Demonstrator MX60 GXB is seen leaving Pontypridd Bus Station during May 2011 on service 100E. It later found homes with Baker Bus and D&G Bus. (Peter Owen)

On demonstration with Edwards is Scania Omnilink YT11 LPN. It is photographed on the 400E service as it leaves Cardiff on 28 June 2011. It later found a permanent home with Xelabus of Eastleigh. (Andrew Wiltshire)

Optare Solo Slimline M880SL demonstrator YG59 GGP is photographed on loan to Edwards, operating service 100E in July 2011. It was later acquired by P&O Lloyd, Bagillt. (Peter Owen)

One of four new to Edwards in 2005 as per the prior advertisement (see p. 55), Setra S315GT-HD BX05 UVU is seen in Burnham-on-Sea on 7 July 2011. BX05 UVU received registration P500 EDW in June 2013 whilst UVR, UVS, UVT became P200/300/400 EDW, respectively. (Mike Street)

Photographed leaving Pontypridd Bus Station is 8.8-metre Alexander Dennis Enviro 200 YX61 BXF in October 2011. It is working service 100E route, branded the 'Ponty Dart'. It was one of three shorter wheelbase examples new to Edwards in September 2011, the other two being YX61 BYB and YX61 BYC. All three passed to Banga Buses, Wolverhampton, in May 2019. (Peter Owen)

Photographed at Cardiff City Stadium on 24 February 2012 is Van Hool Astron T917 BU55 AFC. It was new to Edwards in January 2009, registered BU55 WRU, receiving registration BU55 AFC in January 2010. In April 2023, it would become CA55 MMU prior to export to Ukraine as a support vehicle together with BU55 WRU, new to Parry's as YJ08 NTT. (Mike Street)

Plaxton Paramount Expressliner-bodied Volvo B10M-60 (no rear window) is seen outside the National Museum, Cardiff, on 1 October 2012 whilst on a private hire. It was new to Tayside Travel Services Ltd in 1990, registered H556 WTS. A model of this very coach was produced by Exclusive First Editions in Caledonian Express livery. It passed to Edwards from Sanders, Holt, in October 2010, lasting in their fleet until 2017. (Simon Ingham)

Plaxton Panther-bodied Volvo B12B YN08 DNV at the Riverfront, Newport, on 10 November 2012. It was heading off on a trip to a craft fair in Birmingham and was one of two new to Edwards in 2008, its sister vehicle being YN08 DNX. It was previously Edwards' only dedicated National Express vehicle prior to contract and fleet expansion with the arrival of Caetano Levante-bodied Volvo B9Rs. It was refurbished and re-registered to LUI 7923 during 2024. (Simon Ingham)

Setra S416GT-HD BK09 RLY is seen at the Riverfront, Newport, on a Christmas shopper trip to Bath on 24 November 2012. New to Diamond in 2009, it is still in their livery whilst in Edwards' possession. (Simon Ingham)

Bova Futura FHD12-370 WA03 EYG is seen outside the National Museum, Cardiff, on 12 December 2012. It would receive registration K400 EDW in August 2013 and was one of three new to Edwards in March 2003, the other two being WA03 EYF (K200 EDW) and WA03 EYH (K500 EDW). (Simon Ingham)

MAN 14.220 MCV Evolution AE55 MVC is photographed on service 100E on 29 May 2013. It was new as a dual-doored vehicle to Meteor Parking and was used on the Hilton shuttle service at London Stansted Airport. After its life with Edwards, it passed to Peyton Travel before finally becoming a 'book bus' at Swallowdale Primary School, Melton Mowbray. (G. L. Phillips)

Photographed in the parking area at the Custom House, Cardiff Bay, on 30 June 2013 is ex-Diamond BK09 RLY, by this point painted in the standard Edwards' livery of the time. (Simon Ingham)

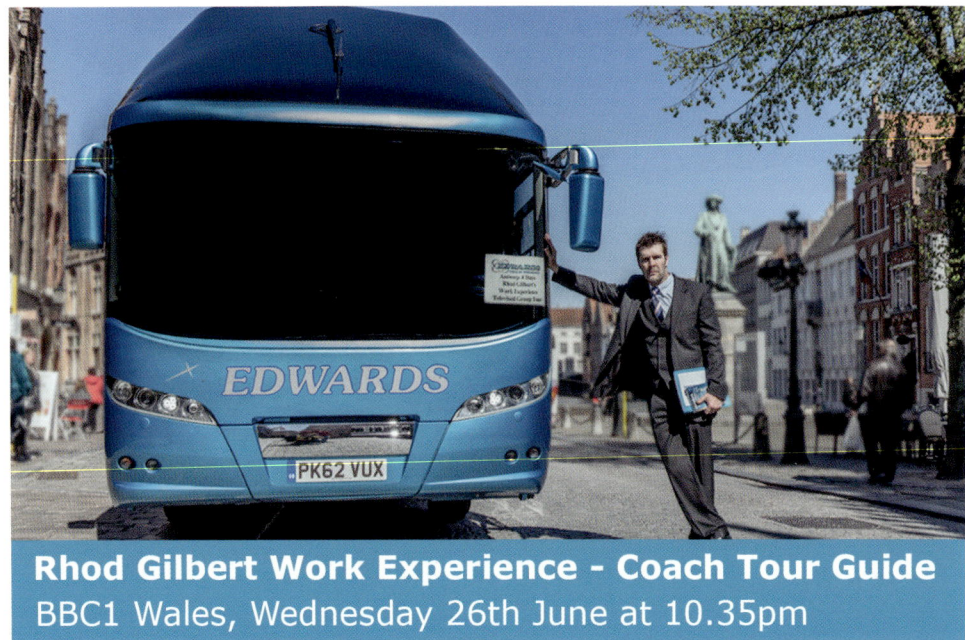

Rhod Gilbert Work Experience - Coach Tour Guide
BBC1 Wales, Wednesday 26th June at 10.35pm

Welsh comedian and television presenter Rhod Gilbert is seen leaning against Neoplan Starliner 2 PK62 VUX during filming for an episode of the BBC's *Rhod Gilbert's Work Experience*. During the episode, which aired on 22 August 2013, he took Edwards' customers on a guided tour of Antwerp and Bruges. PK62 VUX would be re-registered to SOI 196 in November 2018. (Edwards collection)

Working service 100E, Optare Versa demonstrator YJ61 JHF is approaching Pontypridd Bus Station in February 2013. It would end up in the fleet of Lugg Valley Travel, Leominster. Much later, Edwards acquired solitary Optare Versa YJ09 OTS to support local services, but no orders were ever placed for new vehicles of this type. (Peter Owen)

Alexander ALX400 Transbus Trident OHZ 6704 is seen at Park Place, Cardiff, working a university halls' service on 22 January 2014. It was new in June 2002 with East London as LY02 OAS, with fleet number TAS544, later becoming 17544 in the Stagecoach fleet. It was one of three of the type acquired by Edwards, the others being Y8 EDW (SN53 KJV) and TIL 6474 (X278 NNO). (G. L. Phillips)

The dedicated coach for Edwards' educational tours, named '*École*', was Neoplan Tourliner OU14 SUF, seen here when new in 2014. It would later receive standard metallic-blue fleet livery with vinyl indicating its use on educational tours, as well as registration 210 HKT. (Edwards collection)

Setra S416GT-HD BK08 NJU is seen in the now demolished Plymouth Bretonside Bus Station whilst on a Mother's Day excursion to the city from Torquay on 16 March 2014. It would be re-registered to N800 EDW in January 2017, at the same time sister vehicle BK08 NJO would receive N700 EDW. (Simon Ingham)

New to Edwards in September 2005, Sitcar Beluga 2-bodied Mercedes-Benz Vario WJ55 EWD rests alongside Volvo B10-62 Plaxton Panther PVV 315 in the Swansea Depot on 23 March 2014. The latter was new to Shearings as W228 JBN, fleet number 228. It also wore National Holidays livery before passing to Edwards. (Simon Ingham)

Duple 340-bodied Volvo B10M-61 D215 LWX was new to Wallace Arnold in March 1987. It entered the Edwards fleet from McCall, Lockerbie, in March 2010. It is seen in the Llantwit Fardre Depot on 13 July 2014. It was scrapped in early 2016. (Simon Ingham)

New to Fairway Commercials, Appleton, but entering the Edwards fleet from DAC Coaches, St Anne's Chapel, Enterprise Plasma EB03 Plaxton Primo YX60 BZL is photographed in Pontypridd Bus Station on 24 July 2014 wearing 'Ponty Dart' branding for service 100. It arrived with Edwards with similar MX56 NMA from the same source in May 2014, both being withdrawn in 2016. (John Jones)

A selection of Edwards brochures from years gone by, including the ninetieth anniversary brochures from 2015. (Edwards collection)

Plaxton President-bodied Dennis Trident N70 EDW is seen on Greyfriars Road, Cardiff, during March 2015. It was being utilised on the 400 service for its high capacity on a day that Wales were playing Ireland in the Rugby Six Nations. It was new to London General as PJ02 PZM, with fleet number PDL14, and was the only one of this type used by Edwards, albeit PJ02 PZN was also acquired but destroyed by fire and not operated. (Peter Owen)

The line-up of Edwards' 2015 intake of ten Mercedes-Benz Tourismos in front of the Wales Millennium Centre, Cardiff Bay. Closest to the camera is BJ15 BCU. (Edwards collection)

Photographed in the Llantwit Fardre Depot on 2 November 2015 is short-wheelbase Duple-bodied Dennis Javelin WKZ 3537. It was new to Dewar, Falkirk, in October 1989, registered G166 HMS, passing to Edwards from Gregory, Pontyclun, in April 2010. (Simon Ingham)

In its 'Team Wales' livery, Neoplan Starliner 2 ML13 XOB (YAP 104) is photographed at Sophia Gardens on 28 April 2016. It was one of three new to Edwards, the others being PK62 VUX (SOI 196) and ML13 XNZ (PVV 315), all three receiving their cherished plates from November 2018. In March 2024, together with BU55 WRU (BF68 ZDZ), it received the revised 'Red Dragon' livery, in keeping with Mercedes-Benz Tourismo BF73 CDN. (Simon Ingham)

Photographed in Cheltenham Royal Wells Coach Station during July 2016 is Caetano Levante-bodied Volvo B9R FJ11 GMU. It is wearing an overall wrap for the Football Association of Wales with 'diolch' and 'together we are stronger' wording. Identical FJ11 GOH also received the same wrap. Both were new to Edwards for National Express work in 2011. (Adrian Hampton)

Mercedes-Benz Tourismo BJ15 AVZ is photographed in Edwards' Swansea Depot on 26 February 2017. It was one of ten that were new to Edwards in March 2015. (Charlie Osborn)

High-capacity Bluebird school bus SIJ 814 is seen in Edwards' Swansea Depot on 10 March 2017. It was new to Staffordshire County Council in 2000 as W424 VCH and withdrawn during 2016. Affectionately named 'the prison bus' by children it carried to school, it was one of three acquired by Edwards from the same source, the others being W423 VCH and W426 VCH. (Charlie Osborn)

Photographed on a snowy 'Norway-Voss & the Western Fjords' tour on 16 May 2017 is Mercedes-Benz Tourismo BJ15 AVY. It would later become V23 EDW. (Charlie Osborn)

VDL Futura 2 FHD2-129/370 WJ66 KCN is seen at Cardiff West Services picking up customers heading to Eastbourne on 7 August 2017. It would receive registration P444 EDW. It is one of five of the type new to Edwards during 2016, the others being WJ16 KBO, WJ16 KBP, WJ16 KBV and WJ66 KCN. (Simon Ingham)

Bluebird Q school transport vehicle P36 JCR is seen in Llantwit Fardre Depot on 3 August 2017. It was new to West Sussex County Council in September 1996, passing to Edwards via Bakerbus, Royden, in January 2013. (Simon Ingham)

New in March 1989 as F902 YNV to Motts Travel, Stoke Mandeville, Jonckheere Deauville-bodied B10M-60, with registration RIL 1759, is seen in the Llantwit Fardre Depot on 3 August 2017. It entered the Edwards fleet from Laser, Tonypandy, in August 2011 and was withdrawn in August 2018 and scrapped the following year. (Simon Ingham)

UVG UniStar-bodied Dennis Javelins N195 RGD and N245 RGD are seen either side of YN06 CKK in the Llantwit Fardre Depot on 3 August 2017. Both were new to the Ministry of Defence in January 1996 and acquired by Edwards for use primarily as school transport vehicles. (Simon Ingham)

Plaxton Excalibur-bodied Volvo B10M-62 M132 UWY is seen in the Llantwit Fardre Depot on 10 August 2017. New to Wallace Arnold in March 1995, it arrived at Edwards from Arrive in Style, Leeds, in August 2013. (Simon Ingham)

New in June 2008 to London Mini (Isleworth) as WA08 GRZ, Sitcar Marlin-bodied Mercedes-Benz Atego 1022L P16 EDW is seen in Cardiff Bay on a private hire on 20 August 2017. (Charlie Osborn)

Plaxton Verde-bodied Volvo B10B P639 FFC entered the Edwards fleet from Glamorgan Bus in March 2013, yet was new to the Oxford Bus Company in April 1997. It is seen in the Llantwit Fardre Depot alongside ex-Arriva Volvo B10B-58s N588 CKA and N586 CKA with Wright Endurance bodywork on 3 January 2018. Similar but not acquired by Edwards, N592 CKA entered preservation and was restored in Merseybus livery. (Simon Ingham)

A trio of Van Hool T8 Alizee Volvo B10M-60s photographed on 3 February 2018. From left to right: WJI 2858 was new in August 1993 and passed to Edwards via Laser Travel, Tonypandy, in 2008; TIL 1691 was new in February 1993 and passed to Edwards from Kingfisher Travel in 2008; and WIL 8276 was also new in February 1993, coming to Edwards from Cavendish, Llwynypia, in February 2011. (Charlie Osborn)

Neoplan Tourliner OY64 KKE is seen on a 'Green Spain' Tour, appropriately adorned with the Spanish and Welsh flags at the top of the windscreen, on 13 October 2018. It was one of two new in 2014, the other being OU14 SUF. Both followed the purchase of similar PK62 VUW, new in November 2012. (Charlie Osborn)

Berkhof Axial-bodied Dennis Javelin W108 NDE is seen in Port Tennant, Swansea, on 30 May 2019. It was new to Silcox of Pembroke Dock in March 2000 and entered the Edwards fleet as Silcox ceased trading. It was withdrawn during September 2019. (Charlie Osborn)

Plaxton Prima-bodied Dennis Javelin TIL 8238 is seen in the Swansea Depot, its rear advert promoting the Edwards-owned Portbyhan Hotel in Looe, Cornwall, on 10 October 2019. It was acquired from Silcox in 2016, being new to the MoD in 2001, initially registered Y183 SRK and then re-registered to Y154 EBY in July 2014. (Charlie Osborn)

Photographed in Bristol Bus and Coach Station is Caetano Levante-bodied Volvo B9R RIL 1214, new as FJ12 FXU, on 22 December 2019. With its destination display denoting that it is helping out on National Express work, it was operating out of Edwards' Bristol Depot on the 040 service between Bristol and London. It was one of a few to be retained and repainted into Edwards' blue livery after use on the National Express network. (Alistair Rigley)

A sign of the times in 2020. Edwards installed this signage onto vehicles that were used during the Covid-19 pandemic, as seen on this unidentified Setra. Specific instructions to passengers included using the hand gel provided, filling the coach from the rear first and using seats only marked available for use to promote social distancing. (Edwards collection)

Three VDL Bova Magiqs are at Edwards' Llantrisant Depot on 12 June 2020. EOI 4364 stands alongside RJI 8687 and SJI 2449. All three were part of an intake of six new to Diamond in 2008, initially being registered WA08 GOX, WA08 GPV and WA08 GOU, respectively. WA08 GPU also made it into the Edwards fleet but was sold to Vale Cars, Henstridge, in November 2015. Similarly, six of Diamond's 2009 intake of ten VDL Bova Magiqs made it into the Edwards fleet, these being WA09 HTJ/P/T/U/V/X. (Simon Ingham)

Resting in the Llantrisant Depot, 9.7-metre Alexander Dennis Envrio200 MMC YW68 PDO was photographed on 12 June 2020. Note the 'thank you NHS' poster in the windscreen and notices on seats marking them out of use to encourage social distancing during the Covid-19 pandemic. It was one of six new in January 2019, the others being YW68 PDK, YW68 PDU, YW68 PCY, YW68 PCZ and YW68 PCX, the latter being the only 8.9-metre variant. (Simon Ingham)

Three high-specification touring coaches are seen in the Llantrisant Depot on 12 June 2020. Closest to the camera is Van Hool T917 Astron Y8 EDW, formerly YJ11 AOC and new to Parry's International but acquired by Edwards in February 2014. Alongside is Neoplan Starliner 2 YAP 104, previously ML13 XOB, which was new to Edwards in 2013, followed by another Van Hool Astron, BU55 AFC. (Simon Ingham)

On the same date, Enviro 200 YX64 VRW is seen in the Llantrisant Depot. It and YX64 VRW were new to Edwards in October 2014, both passing to Phil Anslow in May 2021. Alongside is King Long XMQ6900 BX14 KPV, new to Edwards in June 2014 and following similar BN63 NYW new in September 2013. (Simon Ingham)

A line-up of Edwards' Ford Transit minibuses in the Llantrisant Depot on 12 June 2020. Alongside others are P333EDW, T700 EDW and T777 EDW, normally used extensively for tour transfer purposes. (Simon Ingham)

Mercedes-Benz Tourismo BJ15 BCU is seen parked in the Newport Bus Depot on 16 October 2020. It was being used as transport for the Scarlets, who were playing against the Dragons at Rodney Parade. The final score was 10–36 in the Scarlets' favour. (Charlie Osborn)

Mercedes-Benz Tourismo V29 EDW (formerly BJ15 AWH) is seen on a Harry Potter Studio tour on 20 August 2021. It is wearing an impressive wrap for the British & Irish Lions. V28EDW (BJ15 AWG) also wore this wrap and was similarly used for team transfers, both reverting to fleet livery afterwards. V29 EDW was unfortunately lost in a fire near Brecon during September 2024. (Charlie Osborn)

Mercedes-Benz Tourismo V23 EDW, formerly BJ15 AVY, is seen outside the popular tourist destination of Bodmin Jail on 12 October 2021. (Charlie Osborn)

BV22 HCD leads a line of newly delivered Volvo B8RLE MCV Evoras to Edwards on 28 April 2022. All would soon receive the revised Edwards local-service livery. (Simon Ingham)

Caetano Levante-bodied Volvo B9R K50 APL is seen in Bristol Bus and Coach Station on 23 June 2022. It was new for National Express work, registered FJ11 GNK, and retained for use in the Edwards fleet. It was one of two painted in the metallic-blue touring livery, the other being FJ11 GNN. (Simon Ingham)

Mercedes-Benz Tourismo V26 EDW was one of the first coaches to receive the refreshed Edwards' touring livery of 2023. It is seen at Aintree during a birthday celebration with Harry Redknapp and friends on Grand National Day, 15 April 2023. (Lee Marsh)

Volvo B7R Plaxton Profile YN08 SOE is seen in Cardiff West Services on 27 July 2023. It was one of two acquired new in June 2008, the other being YN08 SOC. (Simon Ingham)

Photographed on 17 August 2023 is 14.6-metre Van Hool TDX21 Altano NXI 813 at the Vale Hotel. It was new in March 2014 as WA14 DTZ. It won 'Top Touring/Express Luxury Coach' together with the Cymru Trophy for the best coach from Wales at the 2014 UK Coach Rally at Alton Towers. (Charlie Osborn)

Volvo B8RLE MCV Evora BV22 HCF is seen outside the former Western Welsh premises known as 'The Bus Depot', Barry, the home of the Cardiff Transport Preservation Group, on 3 September 2023. Alongside is preserved Cardiff Bus Alexander Dash-bodied Dennis Dart N23 OBO, sister vehicle to N25 OBO and N28 OBO, previously owned by Edwards. The registration plate of N25 OBO is displayed on the wall inside the Barry Depot. (Tudor Thomas)

DAF-engined Irizar i8 BU55 AFC (formerly YT68 LCE) is seen at the Lyon Metropole Stadium on 26 September 2023. It was new to Ferris, Nantgarw, in September 2018 but passed to Edwards via Llew Jones, Llanrwst, in September 2023. (Charlie Osborn)

Scania Irizar i6 YS18 NSK looks fresh having been newly painted into the Edwards livery in September 2023. It was new to KB Coaches of Eastington in July 2018, passing to Edwards in June 2023. (Edwards collection)

Brand new and prior to entry into service, Mercedes-Benz Tourismo BF73 CDE is parked in the Llantrisant Depot on 10 November 2023. The next day it would make its inaugural trip to Disneyland Paris. Note the application of the poppy on its front offside marking Armistice Day and decorative Christmas vinyls in the windscreen for the festive season ahead. (Richard Thomas)

The newest 'Red Dragon' and last of four Mercedes-Benz Tourismos delivered to Edwards in 2023 is BF73 CDN. With forty-seven seats and a centre kitchen, it has two fewer seats than the others of the same type delivered in Edwards' blue livery. Its inaugural trip was to Torquay on 11 December 2023. It is seen exiting the grounds of Hensol Castle on 11 March 2024. This coach won the Mercedes-Benz Best Coach Trophy at the 2024 UK Coach Rally held in Blackpool. (Simon Ingham)

Pictured in the grounds of Hensol Castle on 11 March 2024 during a photoshoot is preserved Plaxton Supreme IV-bodied Bedford YMT JMA 880T. New in May 1979 to Evans, Llanrhaeadr, it passed to Edwards via Bradford, Ystrad Mynach, in June 2009. It was bought for preservation in December 2022 by Stuart and Ann Gerrish. Residing in Brecon, it has frequented a number of transport events in Edwards' blue livery, which it received in place of white in June 2014. (Simon Ingham)

Mercedes-Benz Tourismo BF73 CDK is seen on the Gotthard Pass, Switzerland, during an appropriately named 'Swiss Alpine Spectacular' tour on 22 March 2024. (Charlie Osborn)

On 11 June 2024, Neoplan Tourliner OV24 VNS is at Drayton Manor having made its inaugural trip to the park with identical OV24 VNR. These are the first vehicles in Edwards livery with digital mirrors. (Charlie Osborn)

Former National Express-liveried Volvo B11RT Caetano Levante K500 EDW (BV67 JXU) is one of the first of the type to receive Edwards livery for use primarily on private-hire work. It is captured at Llantrisant depot during October 2024. (Simon Ingham)

National Express vehicles form a large proportion of Edwards' fleet. On its first day in service on 1 April 2016, Volvo B11RT Caetano Levante BX16 CHN is seen leaving Sophia Gardens on an evening 509 service to London. (Simon Ingham)

Named John, BV66 WPK was one of ten Caetano Boa Vistas operated by Edwards' Bristol Depot for use on the 040 service between Bristol and London. It is seen at Durdham Down, Bristol, on 8 March 2023. (Jaroslaw Majczak)

Caetano Levante 3 BV22 VSO adorned with a poppy and a special 'Lest we Forget' message on the destination display at the Bristol Depot on 10 November 2023. Edwards' National Express fleet mainly comprises similar Scania Levante 3As with digital mirrors in 2025. (Richard Thomas)